A Miracle for Sarah

Regine Schindler

Illustrated by
Eleonore Schmid

Translated by
Renate A. Lass-Potter

Abingdon Press
Nashville

SARA LACHT

© for the German original 1984 by Verlag Ernst Kaufmann D-7630-Lahr, West Germany

A MIRACLE FOR SARAH

ISBN 0-687-27044-8

Printed in Germany

Sarai sat alone on a big rock. Sarai was sad.

Sarai watched as the tents were taken down and rolled up. Sarai watched as the animals were tied together with long ropes: goats, sheep, and cattle. Sarai listened as a mother said to her child: "We have to move on. We have to look for new grazing grounds. Our animals cannot find anything to eat here." Another mother said: "Do not be afraid of the trip. Abram will find the way. He leads us well."

Sarai was Abram's wife. For many years she had traveled with her husband. Abram and Sarai came from a country far away. Sarai had left behind her mother and father, her brothers and sisters. She also had left behind her little gods, the idols to whom she had prayed.

"Leave the little idols at home," Abram had told her.

Sarai had been away from home for many years. Sometimes she felt lonely. She was homesick. She wanted very much to stay in one place.

But Sarai loved her husband. She was going farther and farther away with Abram; with his servants; with his goats, sheep, cattle, donkeys, and tents. The others thought Sarai was lucky. She had pretty colored dresses. She had bracelets and the biggest tent. They did not have these things. Sarai was beautiful, too. She was the most beautiful one of all.

"Abram, have the gods shown this way to you?" Sarai asked her husband.

"The gods?" Abram looked at his wife appalled. "No, we no longer need these gods, these little idols. I do not want to worship them any longer. They are lifeless. They never spoke to me."

Sarai asked again: "Abram, where are we going? Why are we going farther and farther away from home? Who showed you the way?"

"God has talked to me, Sarai. He leads us. He will show us a new country. He will make us a great people. He will bless us."

What kind of a God does Abram obey? What does blessed mean? Sarai wanted to ask so much more. She noticed that Abram's face was happy. That made Sarai a little happy, too. It was a good God who talked to Abram, she thought. She moved on with her husband.

During the journey the herds increased in number. Abram became richer and richer. He had many animals. Many servants had to serve him. They all followed him with their families.

Even the pharaoh, the mighty king of Egypt, gave presents to Abram. He gave him donkeys and camels, and servants who spoke in a foreign language.

Abram rested under a big oak tree. He wanted to be alone. He piled up layers of stone very carefully. For a long time he collected the right stones from the field.

Sarai stood nearby. She watched as Abram knelt down. He prayed. He talked and listened. Sarai came closer. She asked, "Abram, are you talking to the God who leads and protects us?" Abram nodded. Abram had piled up stones into an altar for his God. Here he prayed.

Sarai thought: He must be a powerful god—an invisible, mighty god. Perhaps he is mightier than the great pharaoh of Egypt. I would like to know what the invisible god tells Abram.

From under the big tree Abram answered: "God told me he would give this land—the land Canaan—to my children, my grandchildren, and my great-grandchildren. This is a fertile land, where there is enough to eat for everyone."

"How is this possible?" asked Sarai. "We do not have any children," she said sadly.

She was no longer young. She had been waiting for children for a long time. She was embarrassed. I am not a good wife, she thought. A woman who does not have any children is like a tree without fruit. What good is the land that God gives us if I do not have children?

Sarai had colorful dresses. She had bracelets and the biggest tent. In front of her tent lay lovely rugs. Sarai was still very beautiful, but she did not have a child. More than anything else, Sarai longed for a child, a child of her own.

Sometimes Sarai remembered the little idols from home. Other women had those gods and prayed to them. Perhaps they could help more than the invisible god.

The long journey went on. Sarai traveled with Abram through the country for many years. The big tent with the lovely rugs was set up. Then it was taken down again. Abram searched again and again for new places to camp, fresh water, and new grass. All around, the ground was stony and dry. Only thorny shrubs grew.

Again and again Sarai watched Abram pray. Had God talked to him? She did not always want to ask.

One day Abram and Sarai looked into the distance. Abram said: "God has talked to me. He will give us as many children and grandchildren and great-grandchildren as there are dust particles in all this land. We shall move on through this country and travel the length and the breadth of it. It shall belong to our children. God, who has created heaven and earth, protects us. He will help us."

But Abram was often very sad. Will God not help me after all? He has created heaven and earth! He has promised children and grandchildren to me. Why does he not give us a child? Who shall inherit my land and my herds?

Abram's servants had children and grandchildren and great-grandchildren. The donkeys had offspring. The sheep, goats, and cattle had young. The herds that traveled from camp to camp grew in numbers.

But Sarai did not have a child.

Once Sarai woke up in the middle of the night. She was afraid. The place at her side was empty. Abram had left the tent.

She looked through the entrance of the tent, which was half-way open. Abram stood lonely among the little barren bushes. He raised his arms toward the sky. The sky was filled with thousands of blinking stars.

Sarai sat up. She waited until Abram returned. "Has God talked with you?" she asked softly. Abram nodded. "Our people shall be as many as the stars in the sky. They will be our children, grandchildren, and great-grandchildren."

There were countless stars. Sarai sighed, "And I do not have even one child. Abram, take another wife. I cannot have children."

In another tent a baby cried.

"God will make even us happy. He is our friend," whispered Abram and lay down next to Sarai in the tent.

A few days later the journey continued.

They wandered for many years. Sarai got new bracelets and shining chains. She lived in a new tent with beautiful curtains and rugs. Abram's herd grew, and he became richer and richer. Sarai thought of the invisible god. Does he no longer talk with Abram? Can he still help us? She looked at her old wrinkled hands. Abram also was old by now. His hair was white.

One day, when Sarai was kneading dough, she heard strange laughter. She stepped out of the tent. What was her old husband laughing about? He knelt on a little hill. He bent so far forward that his forehead touched the ground. He shook with laughter and then was still for a long time.

He is listening to the invisible God, Sarai thought. Why can I not hear God's voice?

Finally Abram got up. He shook the dust from his clothes. "Have you laughed in front of God?" Sarai asked, surprised.

Abram answered, "God said that we will have a child one year from now. A son. He shall be named Isaac. I had to laugh about this. I am ninety-nine years old, and you are an old woman."

Then Abram got serious again. "God made an agreement with me. He wants us to belong to him completely. With that we become new people and we get new names. I shall be named Abraham—no longer Abram. Abraham means 'Father of Many People'! You, Sarai, belong to the new agreement, too. You also get a new name: Sarah. Sarah means lady, queen. God will bless you, too."

Sarah was astounded. "God is wonderful and strange."

It was noon. The sun shone hot on the tents. The animals seemed paralyzed by the heat. No noise was heard. Everyone was asleep.

Sarah slept way back in the big tent. Abraham lay close to the entrance. Suddenly Sarah was startled by voices. Abraham was already standing. He bowed. There were visitors. Sarah was excited. Who is traveling during this heat? Are those travelers from faraway cities? What will they tell us?

"Please be my guests," Abraham said. Now Sarah saw three men. They sat down in the shade of the big oak tree in front of the tent. This was the place where Abraham built another stone altar for God.

Abraham shook his servant awake and shouted, "Get a basin of water so our guests can wash their feet. They are dusty from the long journey."

And he whispered to his wife, "Take three measures of flour, make dough, and bake bread for our guests." As Sarah started to work, Abraham chose a calf from his herd.

"Slaughter it and prepare it for my guests," he ordered his servants. Abraham went and brought milk for the three men.

Soon flat bread crackled on the hot stones. Sarah watched so that it would not burn. Again and again she looked at the three men.

After the bread was ready Sarah stood behind a curtain close to the entrance of the tent. From here she could watch as Abraham served the guests under the tree. From here she could listen to what they were saying. But nobody could see her.

"Where is Sarah, your wife?" the visitors asked. Sarah quivered. How did the three strangers know her name?

"Inside the tent," Abraham answered. His voice trembled a little.

Then one of the men said: "In about one year I will return. By then your wife Sarah will have a son of her own."

This is laughable, Sarah thought; now I am really too old to have children! And Abraham could already be a great-great-grandfather. She shook her head and laughed.

"I am already like a wilted flower. There is no strength left in me," she told herself.

But then she heard the voice of the visitor saying: "Why is Sarah laughing? Why does she think she is too old to have a child? Does she not know that for God everything is possible? In one year Sarah will certainly have a son."

Sarah was frightened and confused. Anxiously she looked at the three men and said, "I have not laughed."

"Certainly you have laughed," a voice replied.

The men rose and went on their way. Sarah stood still and wondered. Abraham went with his guests for a while. Sarah watched them and said softly to herself: "Now God has talked to me, also."

Then Abraham returned. Now Sarah's eyes began to sparkle. Slowly she smiled. She knew that she, an old woman, would have a child—the child she had been wanting for more than forty years. Now she was happy and she laughed.

Soon Sarah noticed that the child was growing inside her. Her stomach became round. Others noticed it and wondered. Some even laughed: "What an old one she is to be having a baby!"

A boy was born. Abraham named him Isaac as God had told him. Isaac means "God laughs."

Sarah did not forget that she had laughed, too, a long time ago, behind the curtains of the tent. But she was no longer ashamed of that. She knew that God had given Isaac to them. Now their grandchildren and great-grandchildren would live in this country.

She knew for sure. Now the invisible God of Abraham also was her God and her friend.

Sarah prayed to him. "You are a good God," she said. "You have blessed me and I thank you."

She took little Isaac in her arms and cradled him. She was happy. Sarah laughed.

Three years later Isaac could walk and climb. He could talk and sing. He could play with the children of the servants. He could drink and eat by himself. Until now he had nursed from his mother's breasts.

Abraham announced: "Today we will have a feast. We will celebrate Isaac's becoming a strong boy. Soon we can take short trips together." Abraham was proud of his son.

So he invited all his servants and all the children to the feast. It lasted all day, and everybody was happy.